HEADstart

STARS & PLANETS

First published in Great Britain by
CAXTON EDITIONS
an imprint of
The Caxton Book Company,
16 Connaught Street,
Marble Arch, London, W2 2AF.

ISBN 1 84067 056 8

A copy of the CIP data for this book is available from the British Library upon request.

With grateful thanks to Morse Modaberi who designed this book.

Created and produced for Caxton Editions by
FLAME TREE PUBLISHING,
a part of The Foundry Creative Media Company Ltd,
Crabtree Hall, Crabtree Lane,
Fulham, London, SW6 6TY.

Printed in Singapore by Star Standard Industries Pte. Ltd.

HEADstart

STARS & PLANETS

The mystery of outer space, explained in glorious colour

MAUREEN HILL

CAXTON EDITIONS

Contents

Introduction

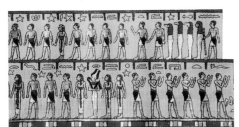

For thousands of years human beings have been fascinated by the skies. In the ancient world, the movement of the stars, planets, sun and moon was important as a way of predicting when the seasons would come and therefore when to plant and harvest crops. The stars in the heavens were also an essential way of navigating, especially at sea. Stonehenge in Wiltshire is thought to be a giant astronomical observatory.

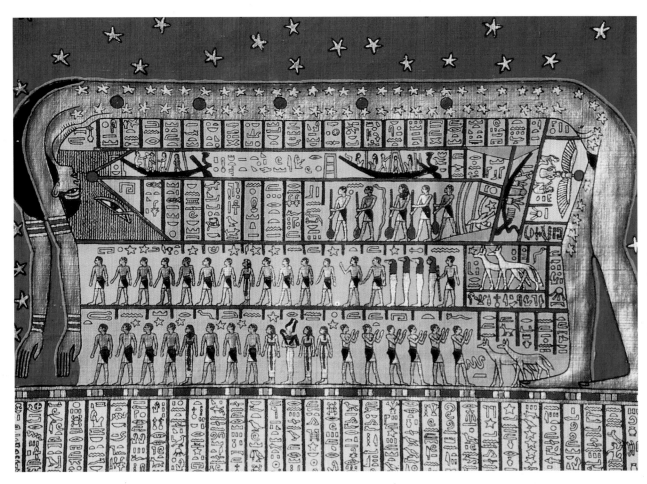

Much early astronomy was involved with naming the stars and finding patterns, or 'constellations'. Astronomy and astrology were closely associated, as many ancient cultures believed that the stars, moon and planets could have an effect on human emotions and destiny.

Since the 17th century, astronomy has developed ever more powerful technology to view the skies. We have been able to send men into space and to our moon. We have sent spacecraft to explore our solar system and beyond. We have learnt much but what we know is only a tiny fraction of what we have still to learn.

We have used the knowledge we have gained to develop theories to try to explain the way the universe came into being and how it works. The most accepted theory is the Big Bang theory: that is the idea that the universe developed from a single point of incredibly dense matter which exploded, releasing the material which created all the galaxies. As a result of this explosion the galaxies, which formed as the universe cooled, after the Big Bang, are still being thrown outward, or expanding.

Whatever the theories, the sky on a clear night, away from the light-pollution of cities and towns, is still a fascinating sight.

Our Solar System

The word 'solar' means 'belonging to the sun' and the sun is the most important thing in our solar system. It has nine planets and an asteroid belt orbiting around it; its gravitational pull keeps the planets in orbit and the mass of the sun – 1,000 times greater than that of all the planets put together – creates its gravity.

The sun is not solid: it is a ball of burning gases. Its core is composed of hydrogen gas which, under the immense heat –

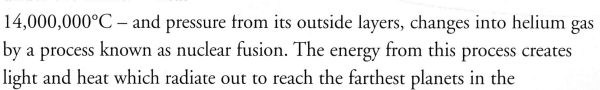

14,000,000°C – and pressure from its outside layers, changes into helium gas by a process known as nuclear fusion. The energy from this process creates light and heat which radiate out to reach the farthest planets in the solar system. The process is not an even one, sometimes flares thousands of kilometres long shoot out into space from the sun. Frequently 'sunspots' appear: this is where magnetic fields cut down the flow of heat and light so that the temperature of the sun's surface 'cools' to 4,000°C – from the average of 5,500°C.

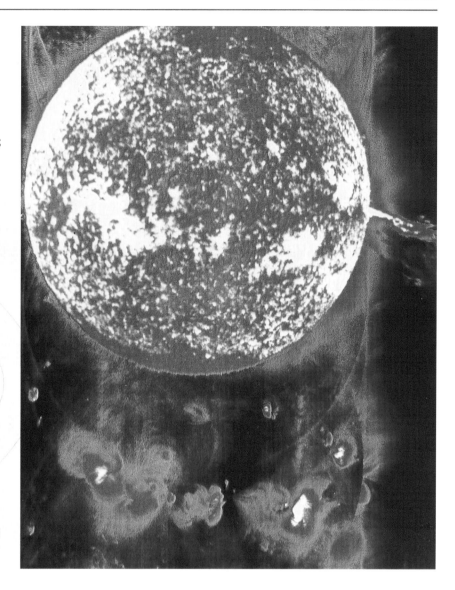

Although the sun uses 500 million tonnes of hydrogen every second, scientists estimate that it is only half way through its life expectancy of 10 billion years!

Like the plants that orbit around it, the sun orbits within our galaxy. It has travelled 23 times around the galaxy in the last five billion years. The sun also spins on its own axis once every 28 days.

The other planets in our solar system are totally dependent on the sun. They are held in position by its gravity, and its heat and light warm their surfaces. The sun also creates an invisible bubble, called the 'heliosphere', which protects the planets from harmful cosmic radiation.

Important – NEVER look directly at the sun, even through sunglasses or a telescope: it can blind you.

Mercury

As the closest planet to the sun, Mercury rises and sets with the sun. For this reason it can only be seen briefly, shining like a star in the east or west, in the twilight of dawn or dusk.

Mercury is a dead world. It has no activity within its core nor volcanoes on its surface, which is marked with many craters. These craters are the result of the impact of debris left over from the creation of the planets. One asteroid in particular was so large that it left a massive crater, called the Caloris Basin. The impact of this asteroid sent shock waves all the way around the planet to the opposite side where the surface was broken up; a huge mountain range was formed as a result.

The planet's atmosphere is millions of times thinner than the Earth's, allowing the temperature to reach 450°C. It is composed mainly of helium and sodium and is patchy, shifting over the planet inconsistentl.

In 1974 the *Mariner 10* spacecraft discovered that Mercury has a magnetic field. This suggests that it must have a large inner core of iron surrounded by a thin layer of rock. The only other way that a planet could generate a magnetic field would be by rotating quickly on its own axis, something Mercury does not do.

Mercury rotates on its axis once every 59 days, whereas it orbits around the sun every 88 days in an elliptical orbit; this means that sometimes the planet can be as close as 46 million km or as distant as 70 million km to the sun. The combination of the planet's rotation and its orbit means that a 'day' on Mercury lasts 176 Earth days.

Venus

Our nearest planet and almost identical in size, Venus is often referred to as Earth's twin, however the conditions on Venus could not be more different from those on our planet. Venus orbits the sun once every 225 days and spins west-to-east on its axis once every 243 days, making a Venusian 'day' as long as 117 Earth days. This west-to-east spin is in the opposite direction to all other planets in the solar system.

The surface is hidden from view by a permanent mass of yellow-orange clouds, composed of sulphuric acid, that travel around the planet every four days. The atmosphere is mainly carbon dioxide, a gas that traps the heat of the sun and heats the planet to 465°C. This is called 'the greenhouse effect' and is an extreme version of what we are experiencing on Earth.

We have built up a picture of the Venusian surface through the observations made by radar projections from Earth, Russian *Venera* spacecraft that landed on Venus and an American spacecraft called *Magellan* which continues to orbit the planet. The surface of Venus is covered with thousands of volcanoes, many of them still active, with pools of lava flowing out of the ground. This volcanic action has covered over any traces of collisions from meteors so, unlike Mercury, there are no craters. Like Mercury, Venus has no water. It is thought that there once was water but that the increased temperature, caused by the greenhouse effect, converted the water into vapour which was lost into space.

Venus was named after the Roman goddess of love. It appears as both the Evening Star and the Morning Star, shining brilliantly at dusk and dawn. Virtually all the land features on Venus are named after famous or legendary women.

Earth

Earth is unique in the solar system: it is the only planet with liquid water and appears to be the only planet that supports life. Life on Earth is supported by the presence of water and Earth's atmosphere, which is composed mainly of oxygen and nitrogen. This atmosphere protects the Earth from harmful solar radiation, excessive heat and impact from meteors.

The Earth's surface is constantly changing. There are huge sections in the Earth's crust, called tectonic plates, which move. This movement creates volcanic action where they meet, as molten rock below the crust comes to the surface. Land surfaces are eroded by the planet's water in the form of seawater, rivers, rainfall and ice.

Below the crust and molten rock is a layer of liquid iron surrounding a solid iron core. This iron and the fast rotation of the Earth generates a strong magnetic field, which shields Earth from harmful solar radiation.

Earth rotates on its axis every 23 hours and 56 minutes; an Earth year lasts 365.26 days. Because Earth's axis is tilted by 23.5°, changes in temperature are created – this is why Earth experiences seasons.

The Moon

The Moon is quarter the size of Earth and one of the largest planets in relation to the parent planet in the solar system. Ocean tides on Earth are influenced by the gravitational pull of the Moon. Similarly, the Earth's gravitational pull has influenced the Moon so that it spins on its axis at the same rate as it takes to orbit the Sun – 27.3 days. This means that only one side of the Moon can be seen from Earth.

We know from our landings and observations that the Moon is a dead and heavily cratered world, but we do not know how it came into being. Was it born with the Earth; is it a chunk broken off the Earth as a result of a collision; or is it a captured asteroid (see page 39)?

Mars

Known as the 'red planet' due toits colour, Mars is the fourth planet in the solar system, which means it is the fourth planet away from the sun. Mars is similar to Earth in that it has volcanoes, canyons, mountains, deserts and icecaps. The biggest volcano in the solar system can be found on Mars: Olympus Mons is 26 km high, three times the height of Mount Everest, and covers an area larger than England with a crater twice the size of London. Like all other volcanoes on Mars, it is believed to be extinct.

In the 19th century, an astronomer named Schiaparelli observed a series of straight, dark lines crossing the surface of Mars. Some people believed these were canals used to irrigate the dry Martian landscape, suggesting that there was life on Mars. However, data

from the two *Viking* crafts sent by NASA (National Aeronautics and Space Administration) has shown that the 'canals' are actually an optical illusion created when the dark rocks lose their covering in sandstorms.

Mars is just over half the size of Earth. A Martian day is only 41 minutes longer than an Earth day but a year on Mars is nearly double an Earth year – 687 days. As its axis is tilted to 25.2°, Mars' temperature fluctuates and it also has seasons. Through a good telescope it is possible to watch the Martian polar icecaps change size with the seasons. These icecaps are made up of carbon dioxide and water but the water never thaws – it is the carbon dioxide ice that melts during the warmer seasons.

The Martian atmosphere is very thin, composed mainly of carbon dioxide with nitrogen and argon. This makes Mars a cold planet: the temperature can vary from -120°C to +25°C.

Mars is orbited by two small, potato-shaped moons, Phobos and Deimos. They are both thought to be asteroids captured by Mars' gravitational pull.

Jupiter

Bigger than all the other planets put together, Jupiter has a small, very hot (35,000°C) rocky core but has no solid crust; it is composed mainly of hydrogen and helium. In the atmosphere above Jupiter the hydrogen is a gas but below this, pressure from the outer layers turns the hydrogen into a liquid form and then into a metallic form. If the planet were 50 times bigger this pressure would cause the hydrogen to fuse and Jupiter would become a star.

Jupiter spins on its axis every 9 hours 55 minutes – faster than any other planet. This spin creates a strong magnetic field, causing the equator to bulge outward, this gives the planet an oval shape.

Jupiter's orbit is beyond the asteroid belt. It circles the sun every 11.9 years, demonstrating how much further out Jupiter's orbit is from the four planets within the belt: Mercury, Venus, Earth and Mars.

In Jupiter's Southern Hemisphere is the Great Red Spot. This is three times the size of the Earth and thought to be a huge storm. Winds spiral upwards, carrying gases to great heights in the atmosphere, where they react with sunlight. This causes them to release phosphorus which produces the red colour. Although it sometimes fades, the spot has remained a permanent feature since it was first observed by Robert Hooke in 1664.

Jupiter is orbited by 16 moons, the largest are: Ganymede, Io, Europa and Callisto. These moons are also known as the Galilean moons after the Italian astronomer Galileo Galilei, who discovered them in 1610. The other moons are all much smaller and the four outermost moons orbit Jupiter in the opposite direction to the others, suggesting they are actually asteroids captured from the asteroid belt by the planet's gravitational pull. In 1979, the *Voyager* spacecraft discovered two faint rings around Jupiter.

Saturn

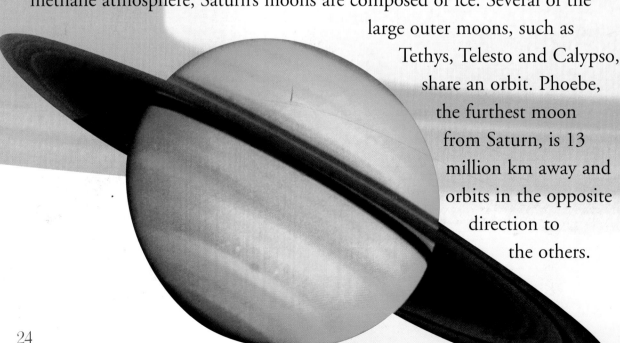

Saturn is a rather featureless planet, except for its beautiful and vivid rings. These are made of pieces of ice and rock and range from the size of a pebble to the size of a small house, perhaps the remains of a moon that shattered when it came too close to the planet.

Three rings are visible from Earth but there are actually seven. Until the visit of the *Voyager* spacecraft, in the 1970s it was believed that Saturn's rings were separated by divisions, such as the Cassini Division, but it has now been discovered that these 'divisions' are actually particles that are less densely packed than the higly visible rings and so are very faint.

Within the rings and beyond, Saturn is orbited by at least 18 moons. Apart from Titan, the largest and one that has its own nitrogen and methane atmosphere, Saturn's moons are composed of ice. Several of the large outer moons, such as Tethys, Telesto and Calypso, share an orbit. Phoebe, the furthest moon from Saturn, is 13 million km away and orbits in the opposite direction to the others.

Although it is smaller than Jupiter, Saturn is very similar in composition: mainly made up of hydrogen in gas, liquid and metallic forms, and some helium. However, despite being the second largest planet, Saturn is very light – it would float in water!

Like Jupiter, Saturn spins very fast: once every 10 hours and 40 minutes. The planet is tilted to 26.7° which means that we get a varied view of the surface of its rings as it completes its 29.5 year orbit of the sun.

Uranus

Uranus was the first planet to be discovered after the invention of the telescope. In 1781, amateur astronomer William Herschel was surveying the sky with his telescope when he spotted a greenish disc. His first thought was that it was a comet but its movement soon showed that it was a planet twice as far away as Saturn. Later astronomers were able to tell that it was another enormous gas planet, smaller than Jupiter or Saturn but four times larger than Earth.

Oberon, Titania, Umbriel, Ariel and Miranda were the only known moons of Uranus, until the visits of the *Voyager* spacecraft in the 1970s. *Voyager 1* discovered a further 10 moons, all of which are much smaller and closer to Uranus than the others. The spacecraft also discovered a series of faint rings, like those around Saturn and Jupiter.

Uranus is a featureless planet that spins on its axis every 17 hours and 14 minutes. *Voyager 2* got photographs of only a few small clouds, moving rapidly through an atmosphere that is composed of methane, hydrogen and helium. Below this atmosphere is a mixture of water, ammonia and methane gases, which cover a rocky core.

One of the most unusual features of Uranus is the 98° tilt of its axis. It is thought to have been hit by an object the size of Jupiter and knocked on its side. This means that the planet spins almost horizontally in space; therefore, as it takes 84 years to orbit the sun, each of its poles has 42 years of sunlight followed by 42 years of darkness. Despite this long exposure to light and dark, Uranus is so far from the sun that there are only a few degrees of difference in temperature between the dark and the light sides, these average about -210°C.

Neptune

It was mathematical calculation that led to the discovery of the eighth planet in the solar system, Neptune. Astronomers first noticed that Uranus was being pulled off course by an unknown gravitational force; it was thought that it could be another planet. Two astronomers, John Couch Adams and Urbain Leverrier, independently calculated where that planet should be, and in 1846 another astronomer, Johann Galle, discovered it, exactly where it had been predicted.

Little was known of Neptune before *Voyager 2* flew by in 1989. Two moons – Triton, the coldest body in the solar system at -235°C, and Nereid – had been seen from Earth but *Voyager 2* discovered six more. The largest of these new moons is Proteus which, like most moons in the solar system, is heavily cratered. *Voyager 2* also discovered a series of four rings – two broad and two thin – around the planet.

Only three per cent smaller than Uranus, Neptune is known as its twin, although it is tilted at 29.6°, not as dramatically as Uranus. Neptune rotates every 16 hours and 7 minutes, making its day 67 minutes shorter than Uranus'. However Neptune takes almost twice as long as Uranus to orbit the sun – doing so once every 165 years.

The surface of Neptune is a mixture of warm water and ammonia and methane gases, which cover a small, rocky core. The atmosphere is composed of hydrogen, helium and methane.

Hurricane winds of up to 2000 km per hour speed across the planet moving clouds of methane ice in the opposite direction to its rotation. There are several storm systems on Neptune: one the size of Earth is named the Great Dark Spot.

Pluto

After the discovery of Neptune it was realised that the planet's mass was not enough to explain the effect on Uranus's orbit. Another, ninth, planet must be affecting it. The hunt for that planet took 75 years. In 1930 Clyde Tombaugh discovered a small planet beyond Neptune. This planet was named Pluto. Its moon, Charon, which is half the size of Pluto was discovered in 1978.

The relationship between Pluto and Charon is extremely close. Pluto rotates on its axis every 6 days and 9 hours – which is exactly the same as Charon's orbit of the planet. Both Pluto's and Charon's axes are tilted at 57.5°. They appear locked together; their movements synchronised.

Pluto is so far from the sun that it takes 248 years to complete an orbit but it has an elliptical orbit and, for 20 years of its long orbit, it enters inside the orbit of Neptune.

Pluto is so far from Earth that no spacecraft has ever visited it, as a result there is a great deal that we do not know about the smallest planet. We do know that it is denser than the gas giants, which means that it probably has a large rocky core with an icy mantle. Its atmosphere contains methane and, probably, nitrogen.

The discovery of Pluto does not answer all astronomical questions: it is believed that the gravitational force of Pluto, Charon and Neptune are still not enough to pull Uranus off course. Because of this many astronomers propose that there is a tenth planet, known as Planet X.

Planet X is speculated to be about the same size as Neptune but twice as far away as Pluto. It is also suggested that Planet X's orbit is at right angles to the orbit of all the other planets in the solar system.

Life of a Star

Stars are born within nebula, that is dark clouds of gas and dust particles which gather together. Once a cloud reaches a certain mass it will collapse in on itself; the pressure from this will cause further contraction until it is a dense spinning ball. The pressure from the mass causes the gases to heat up and a protostar is formed. When the temperature of a protostar's core reaches 10,000,000°C it begins to generate heat and light by nuclear fusion; it then becomes a proper star.

The best known nebula is the constellation in Orion. Although all nebula are revealed best through infra red light, the Orion nebula can also be viewed through binoculars.

From its birthplace in the nebula the star will drift out into space and shine steadily. Astronomers have identified different types of star: blue-white stars, like Sirius, are the largest, hottest and brightest but use their fuel more quickly than stars like our own Sun which glow yellow-orange. Red Dwarf stars, like Proxima Centauri, are the smallest, coolest and dimmest but they will burn for much longer, perhaps for 60 million years.

Stars die because they run out of fuel. As the fuel runs out the star expands and becomes a Red Giant. Smaller stars lose their outer layers and are left with a dead core – a White Dwarf which gradually fades to black. Large stars die with a huge explosion, this is called a 'supernova'. Their remains are thrown out into space and become the building blocks for new stars. However, sometimes a neutron star, which sends out pulses of light and radio waves, or a Black Hole, which is so dense that not even light can escape from it, is left behind.

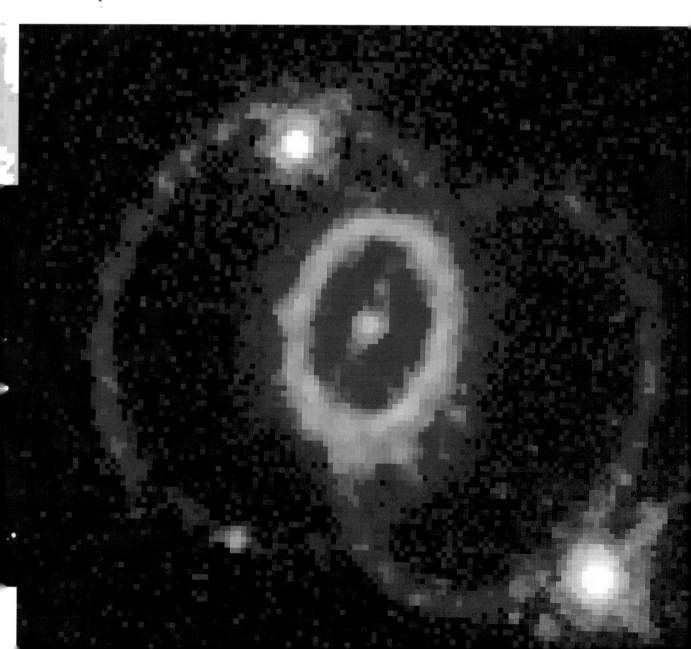

Nearby Stars

The nearest star to our solar system is Proxima Centauri. It is 40 billion km away and it would take a commercial aircraft 5 million years to reach it. The distances between stars are so vast that the distance is measured in light years. A light year is the distance it takes light to travel in a year. Light travels at 300,000 km per second which means that in a light year it would cover 9.5 billion miles. This means that it takes 4.2 light years for the light from Proxima Centauri to reach Earth. The light from our sun takes just over 8 minutes to reach us. The light that we see today from Proxima Centauri came from the star many years ago.

Proxima Centauri is actually part of a triple star system, along with Alpha Centauri A and Alpha Centauri B. Single stars, like our sun, are less common than multiple stars but binary (or two) star systems are most common. The brightest star in the sky, from the viewpoint of Earth, is Sirius, which is 8.6 light years away. Sirius is a binary star with a large bright star named Sirius A and Sirius B. Sirius B is also known as the 'Pup', it is a White Dwarf, the remnant of a dying star.

The nearest star to us which may have planets orbiting it is Barnard's star, which is 5.9 light years away. Although no such planets can be seen from Earth, astronomers have noticed that Barnard's star appears to be influenced by the gravitational pull of at least two other bodies, which suggests the presence of orbiting planets.

The Galaxies

A galaxy is a grouping of millions of stars. Astronomers have noticed that there are different shaped galaxies. There are 'spiral galaxies', in which arms spiral out from a central hub; within this category there are also barred spiral galaxies where the hub is a bar shape. Some galaxies are classified as 'elliptical' and range in shape from almost spherical to a flattened cigar shape. For some galaxies it has not been possible to notice any structure and these are classified as 'irregular'.

Our galaxy is called the Milky Way (the word 'galaxy' comes from a Greek word for 'milky'). It is a spiral galaxy and contains billions of stars. The overall diameter is about a million light years across. Our sun is roughly 32,000 light years from the centre of the galaxy and, like all the other stars within it, the sun orbits around its centre. What is at the centre of the galaxy is unknown but some scientists have suggested that there may be a gigantic Black Hole.

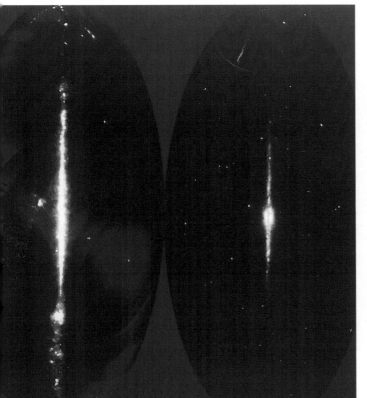

Observations have shown that galaxies are grouped into clusters. The Milky Way belongs to a cluster of about 30 galaxies called the Local Group. The Andromeda Galaxy is the largest galaxy in the Local Group. Even though it is more than 2 million light years distant it is still visible with the naked eye, especially on dark autumn nights in the northern hemisphere.

These clusters of galaxies are further grouped into superclusters. The Local Group is part of a supercluster based around the Virgo cluster.

Comets, Meteors and Asteroids

Comets are magnificent objects, however, they are little more than a snowball in space. Comets have a core of rock or iron but more than half their size (usually only a few kilometres in diameter) is made up of ice. As the comet approaches the sun it evaporates and the solar wind forces the vapour into a tail which streams out behind it.

Comets are unpredictable and can appear at any time. Non-periodic comets take millions of years to complete their orbit; long-period comets have an orbit of at least 200 years. Comets trapped within the gravity of the planets are short-period comets. Halley's Comet visits the inner solar system once every 76 years. Comet Encke orbits the sun in just over three years.

Comets carry waste material around with them. When they fly by a planet some of this material is caught in the planet's gravity and the material falls to Earth as a meteor shower. As they fall to Earth, the meteors appear to be shooting stars. There are regular meteor showers on Earth, the most spectacular is the Perseids in mid-August.

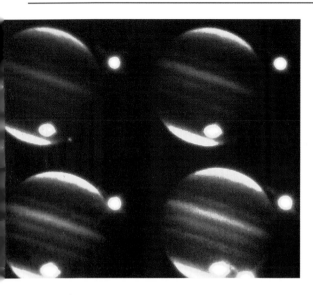

Asteroids are larger than meteors but too small to be called planets. They can be found in large numbers in the Asteroid Belt between Mars and Jupiter. The asteroid belt is thought to be the remains of a planet that has been destroyed, the particles of which were caught within the sun's gravitational pull.

Some asteroids are caught in a planet's gravitational pull, and become moons. If they are not caught within the gravitational pull of a larger body asteroids are free to roam the galaxy.

Exploration

Humans have explored space for thousands of years. For most of that time exploration was by observation with the naked eye. The invention of the telescope in the early 17th century and Galileo's adaptation for its use in astronomy allowed for more detailed observation of the heavens.

Larger and larger telescopes were built, allowing astronomers to see further, and scientists began to realise that there were other ways in which we could 'see' objects in the universe. Infrared and radio telescopes have become important tools of astronomy; as have telescopes on satellites in space. Free of the Earth's atmosphere, the Hubble telescope can produce images of objects that are billions of light years away.

In 1961, Russian cosmonaut Yuri Gagarin became the first human in space and, during the 1960s, the USA and the former USSR sent unmanned spacecraft to explore the Moon. In June 1969, Neil Armstrong and Buzz Aldrin, two of the crew of *Apollo 11*, finally set foot on the Moon. However the Moon landings are the limit of manned exploration in space so far.

Exploration of space continues with unmanned spacecraft like the *Voyager, Pioneer, Ulysses* and *Magellan* probes. Sophisticated communications equipment on board sends back information from the solar system. There are also regular manned missions to orbiting space stations; these continue to undertake scientific experiments, make astronomical observations and to collect information about how space affects human beings. This information will be used when preparing for the next stage of manned exploration; the most likely destination is Mars.

Is Anyone out There?

Earth is the only place in the universe on which we know there is any form of life, let alone intelligent life. We are virtually certain that there is no life on any of the planets in our solar system and, as yet we have not found a planet around any other star. But, given the size of the universe and the billions and billions of stars it contains, it would seem probable that there is life elsewhere. Whether we could ever communicate with these alien life forms is another matter, however.

Radio astronomers concentrate on looking for radio signals from extra-terrestrial intelligent life forms. Of course we have no way of knowing that an alien civilisation would even use radio waves. We do know that the waves from Earth's first radio and television broadcasts have leaked into space; in the vacuum of space the waves travel at the speed of light. By now they will have travelled to the outer edges of our galaxy.

In 1974, a message was sent from the world's largest radio telescope at Arecibo, Puerto Rico. The message used a mathematical code and was targeted on a galaxy 25,000 light years away. This was the first attempt to send a deliberate communication from Earth. Since then many unmanned spacecraft have included devices for communicating with intelligent life, if they ever come into contact with any! The *Pioneer* spacecraft have a plaque on them with a picture of a man and a woman and a map of how to find Earth; *Voyager 1* and *Voyager 2* carry recordings of sounds from Earth, including greetings in many languages. All these spacecraft are travelling out beyond our solar system.

Further Information

Places to Visit

Armagh Planetarium, College Hill, Armagh BT61 9DB. Telephone: 01861 523689.

Jodrell Bank Science Centre, Macclesfield, Cheshire SK11 9DL. Telephone: 01477 571339. Includes a planetarium.

City of Liverpool Museum, National Museums and Galleries on Merseyside, William Brown Street, Liverpool L3 8EN. Telephone: 0151 207 2001. Has a planetarium show.

London Planetarium, Marylebone Road, London NW1 5LR. Telephone: 0171 935 0200.

Natural History Museum, Cromwell Road, London SW7 5BD. Telephone: 0171 938 9123. The Earth Galleries tell the story of Earth from the Big Bang and the creation of the universe up to today.

Old Royal Observatory, Greenwich Park, Greenwich, London SE10 9NF. Telephone: 0181 858 4422. Displays of astronomical instruments and documents, together with information about early astronomy and astronomers.

Royal Observatory, Blackford Hill, Edinburgh EH9 3HJ. Telephone: 0131 668 8100. Focuses on modern astronomy, including displays of two large modern telescopes.

Web Sites

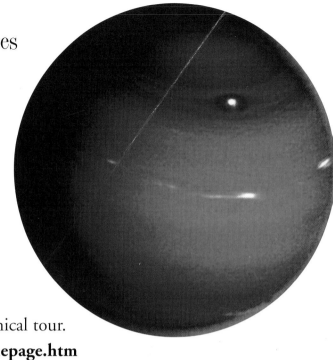

www.nasa.gov
National Aeronautics and Space
Administration (NASA) website.
Information about space exploration and
links to other homepages
of interest.

www.roe.ac.uk
Royal Observatory at Edinburgh's website.
Has good astronomical images.

www.eia.brad.ac.uk/btl/sg.html
Stars and galaxies website – an astronomical tour.

http://servant.geol.cf.ac.uk/solar/homepage.htm
Views of the solar system.

www.nmsci.ac.uk/online/index.html
The Science Museum's website, focusing particularly on the
exploration of space. Also has online exhibits.

Picture Credits

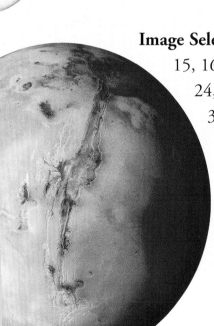